FOR ORGANS, PIANOS & ELECTRONIC KEYBOARDS

E-Z PLAY TODAY

43

Disney

ENCANTO

Music from the Motion Picture Soundtrack
Original Songs by Lin-Manuel Miranda

2 The Family Madrigal

12 Waiting On A Miracle

20 Surface Pressure

34 We Don't Talk About Bruno

44 What Else Can I Do?

29 Dos Oruguitas

52 All Of You

64 Colombia, Mi Encanto

68 Two Oruguitas

ISBN 978-1-70516-364-1

For all works contained herein:
Unauthorized copying, arranging, adapting, recording, internet posting, public performance,
or other distribution of the music in this publication is an infringement of copyright.
Infringers are liable under the law.

E-Z Play® Today Music Notation © 1975 by HAL LEONARD LLC
E-Z PLAY and EASY ELECTRONIC KEYBOARD MUSIC are registered trademarks of HAL LEONARD LLC.

Visit Hal Leonard Online at
www.halleonard.com

Contact us:
Hal Leonard
7777 West Bluemound Road
Milwaukee, WI 53213
Email: info@halleonard.com

In Europe, contact:
Hal Leonard Europe Limited
42 Wigmore Street
Marylebone, London, W1U 2RY
Email: info@halleonardeurope.com

In Australia, contact:
Hal Leonard Australia Pty. Ltd.
4 Lentara Court
Cheltenham, Victoria, 3192 Australia
Email: info@halleonard.com.au

The Family Madrigal

Registration 10
Rhythm: Latin or Salsa

Music and Lyrics by
Lin-Manuel Miranda

5

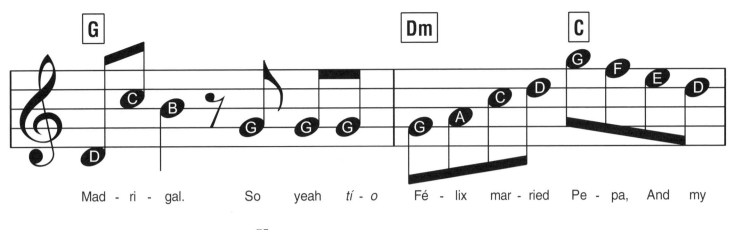

Mad - ri - gal. So yeah *tí - o* Fé - lix mar - ried Pe - pa, And my

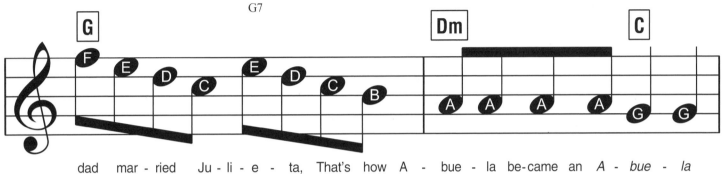

dad mar - ried Ju - li - e - ta, That's how A - bue - la be - came an *A - bue - la*

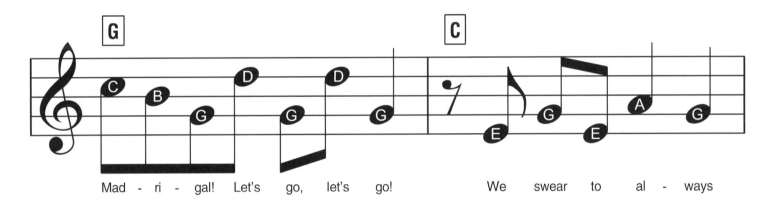

Mad - ri - gal! Let's go, let's go! We swear to al - ways

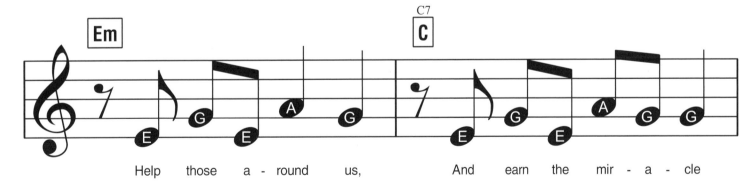

Help those a - round us, And earn the mir - a - cle

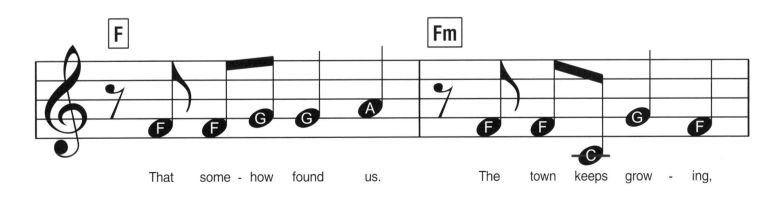

That some - how found us. The town keeps grow - ing,

7

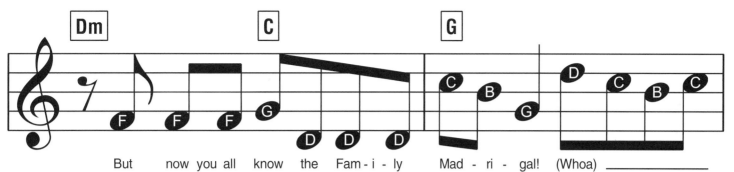

But now you all know the Fam-i-ly Mad-ri-gal! (Whoa) _____

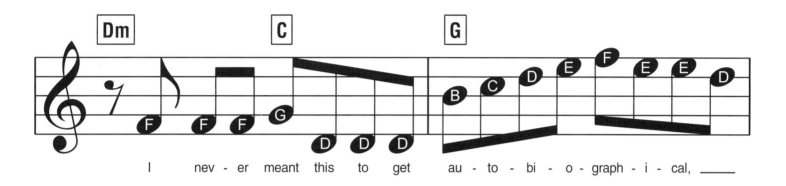

I nev-er meant this to get au-to-bi-o-graph-i-cal, ____

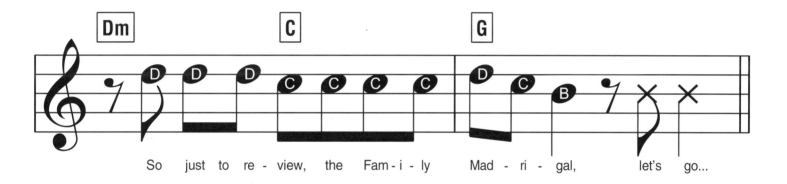

So just to re-view, the Fam-i-ly Mad-ri-gal, let's go...

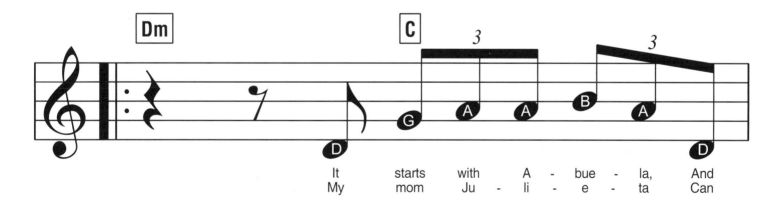

It starts with A - bue - la, And
My mom Ju - li - e - ta Can

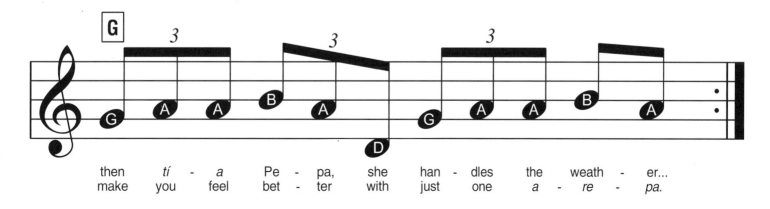

then tí - a Pe - pa, she han - dles the weath - er...
make you feel bet - ter with just one a - re - pa.

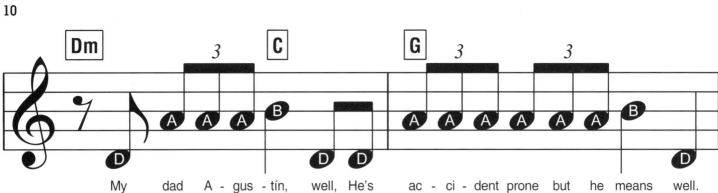

My dad A - gus - tín, well, He's ac - ci - dent prone but he means well.

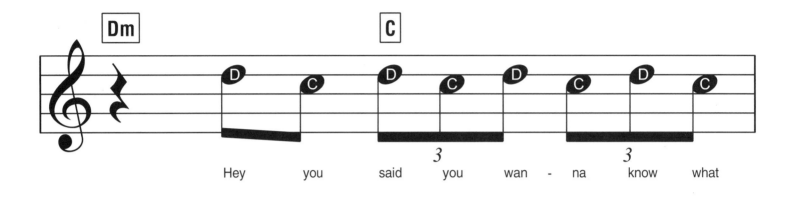

Hey you said you wan - na know what

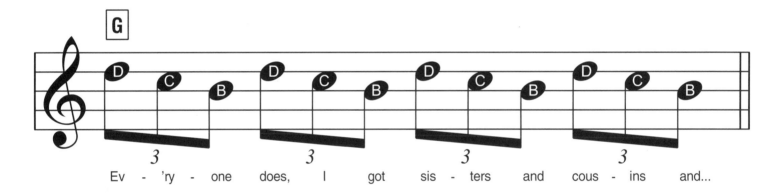

Ev - 'ry - one does, I got sis - ters and cous - ins and...

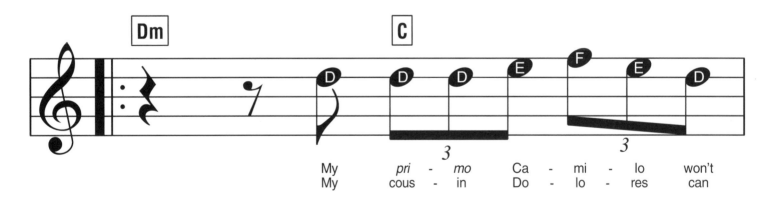

My *pri - mo* Ca - mi - lo won't
My cous - in Do - lo - res can

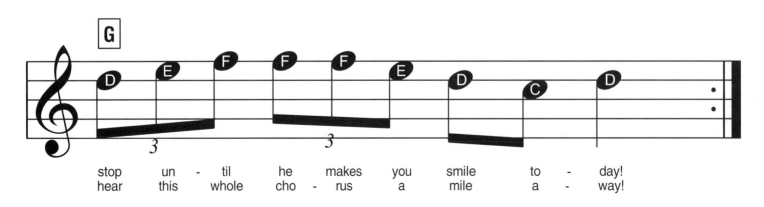

stop un - til he makes you smile to - day!
hear this whole cho - rus a mile a - way!

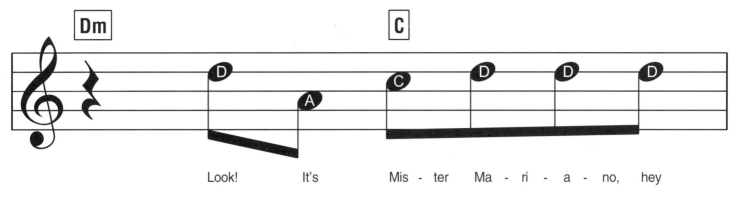

Look!   It's   Mis - ter   Ma - ri - a - no,   hey

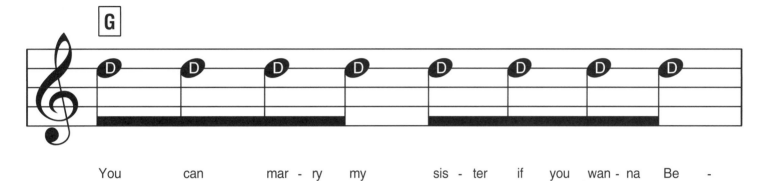

You   can   mar - ry   my   sis - ter   if   you   wan - na   Be -

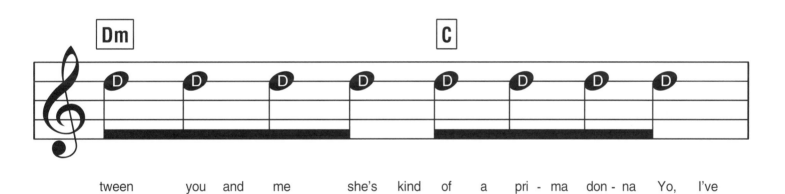

tween   you   and   me   she's   kind   of   a   pri - ma   don - na   Yo,   I've

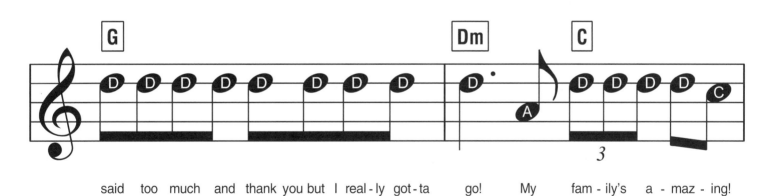

said   too   much   and   thank you   but   I   real - ly   got - ta   go!   My   fam - ily's   a - maz - ing!

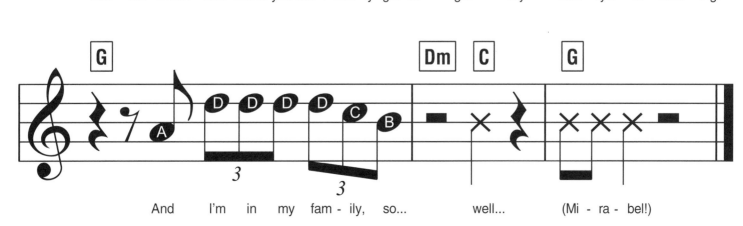

And   I'm   in   my   fam - ily,   so...   well...   (Mi - ra - bel!)

Waiting on a Miracle

Registration 4
Rhythm: Waltz

Music and Lyrics by
Lin-Manuel Miranda

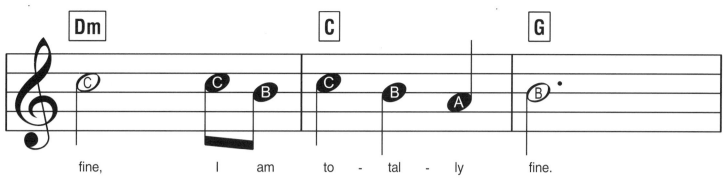

fine, I am to - tal - ly fine.

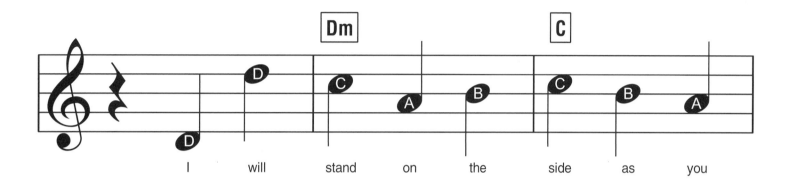

I will stand on the side as you

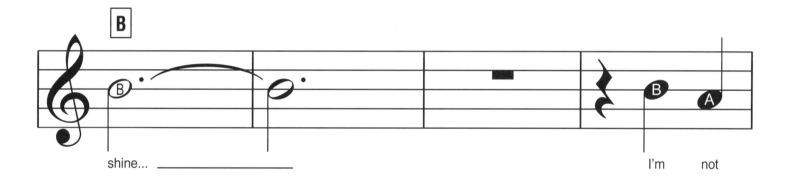

shine... I'm not

B7

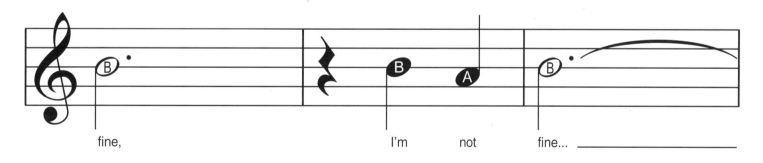

fine, I'm not fine...

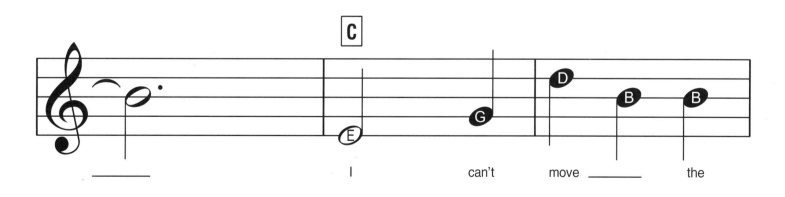

I can't move the

14

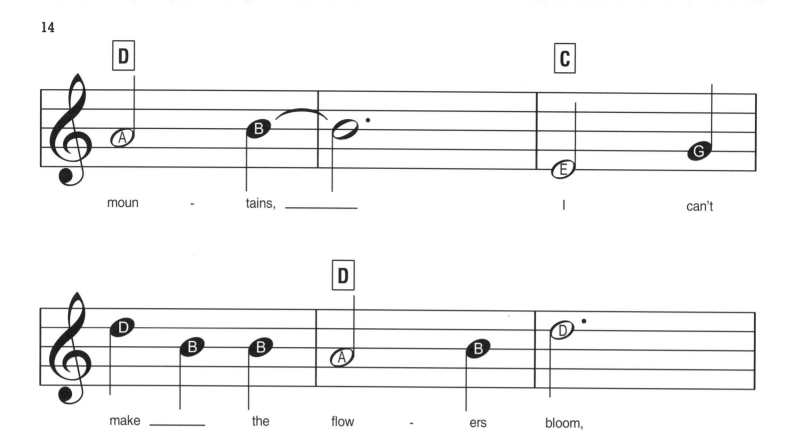

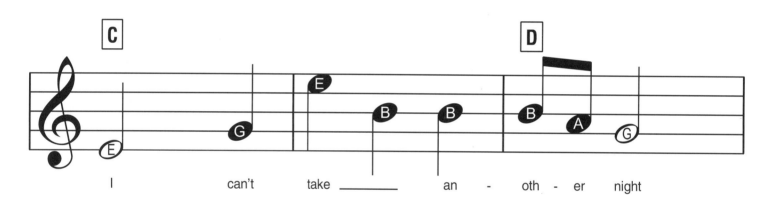

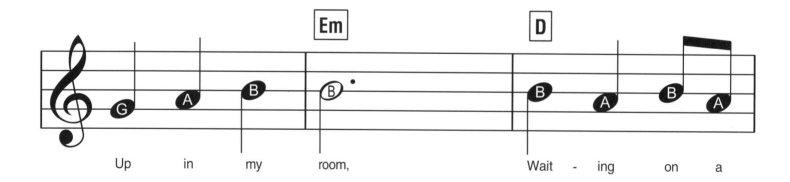

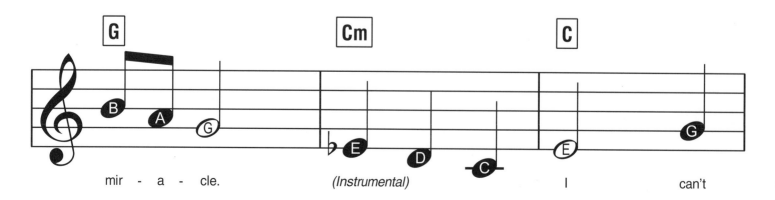

15

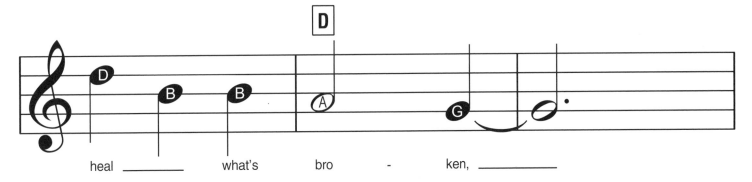

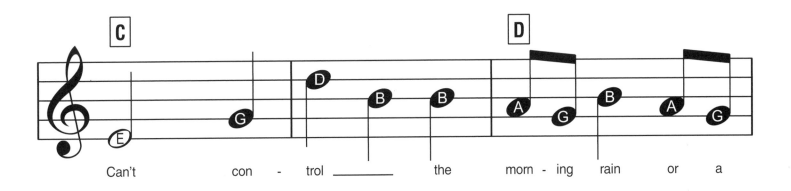

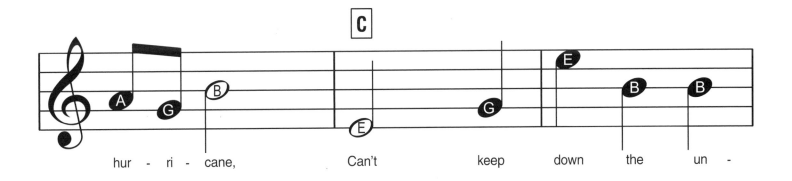

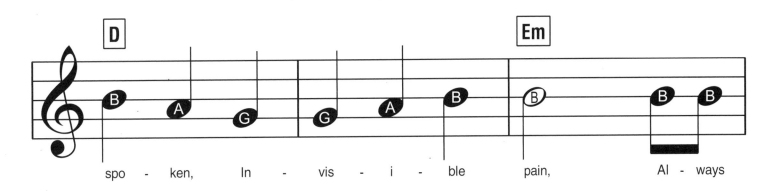

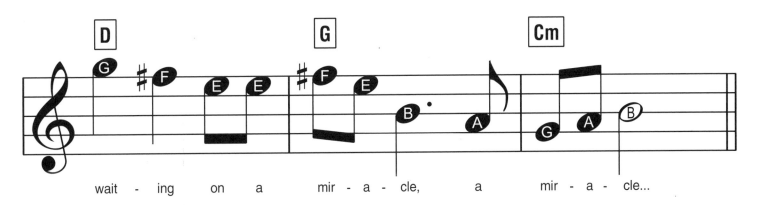

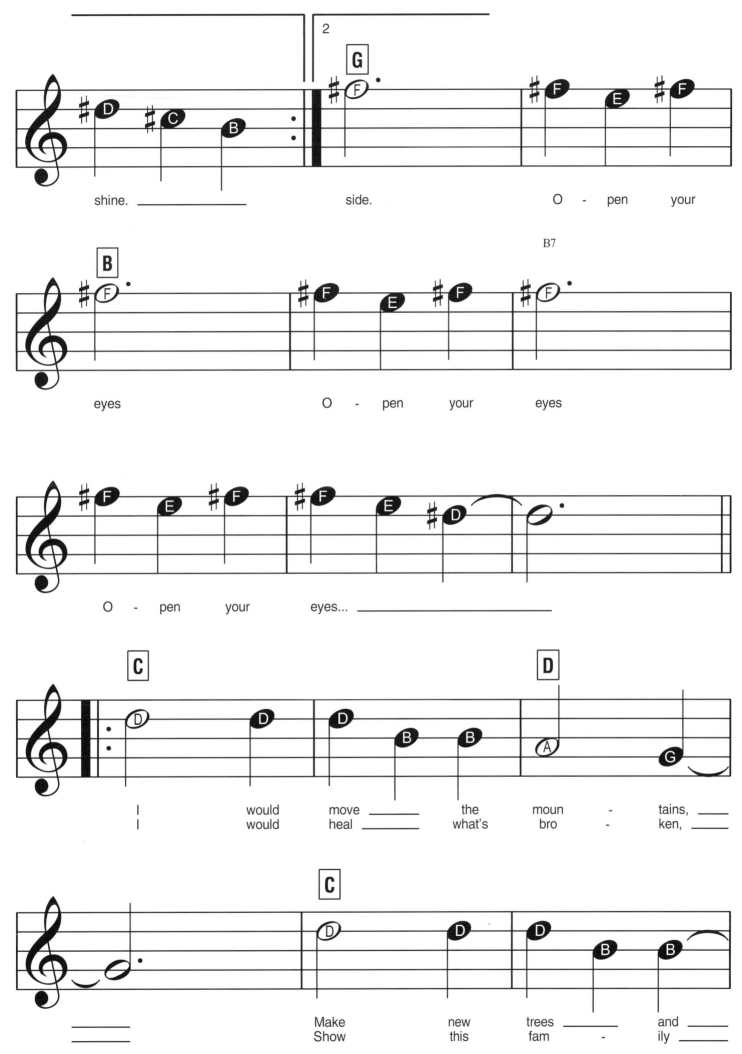

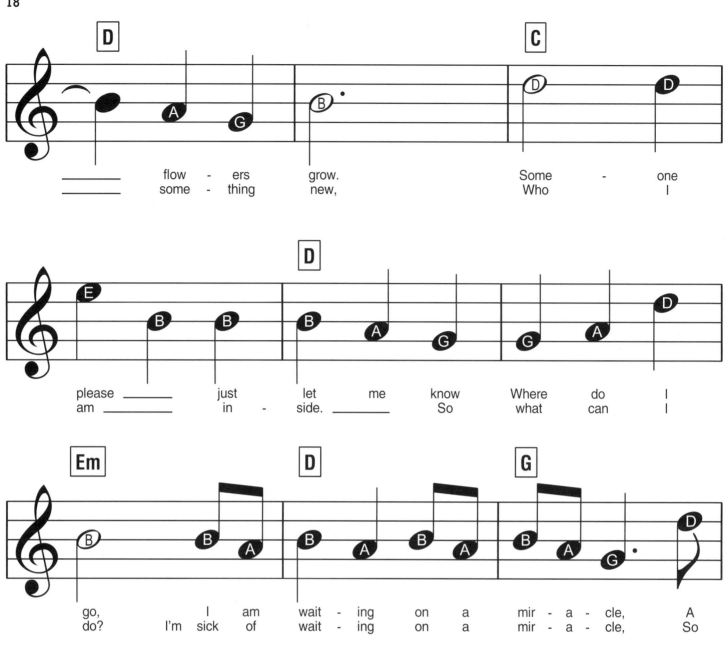

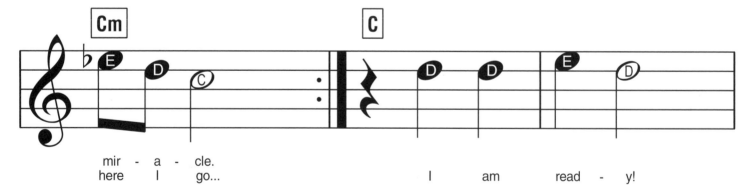

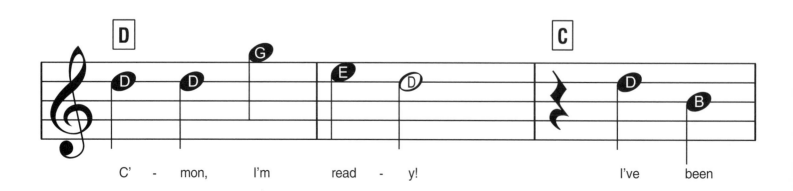

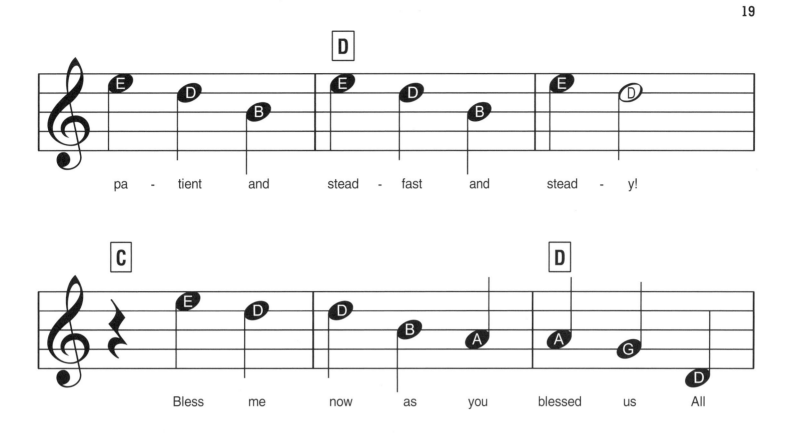

pa - tient   and   stead - fast   and   stead - y!

Bless   me   now   as   you   blessed   us   All

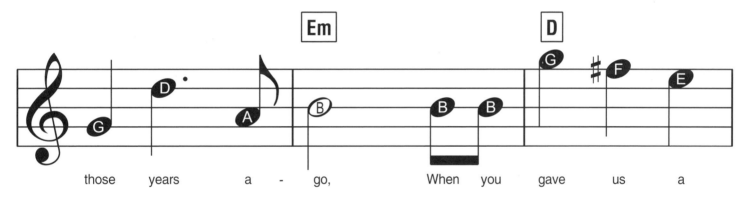

those   years   a - go,   When   you   gave   us   a

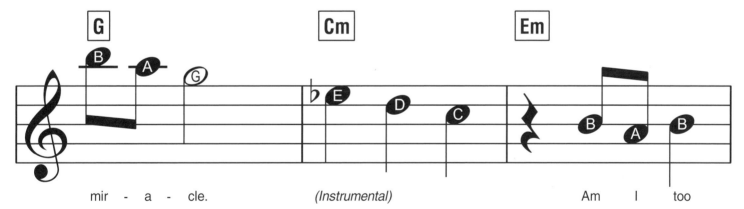

mir - a - cle.   (Instrumental)   Am   I   too

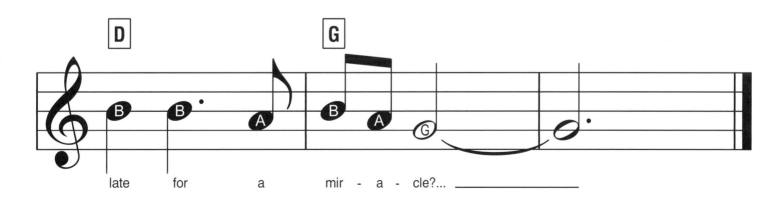

late   for   a   mir - a - cle?... _____

Surface Pressure

Registration 9
Rhythm: Techno Pop

Music and Lyrics by
Lin-Manuel Miranda

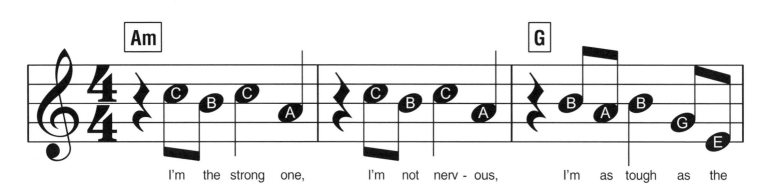

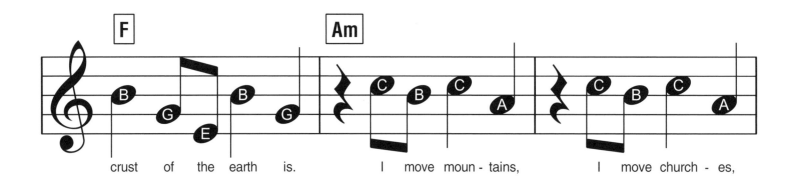

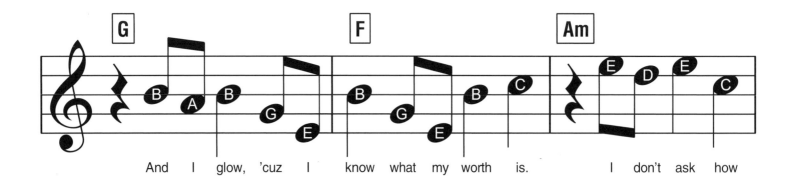

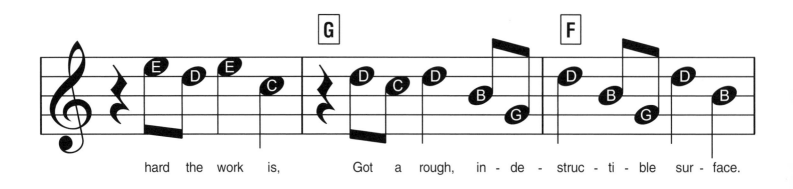

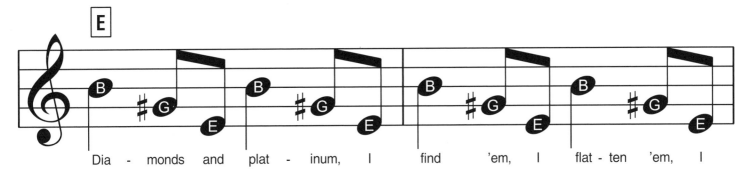

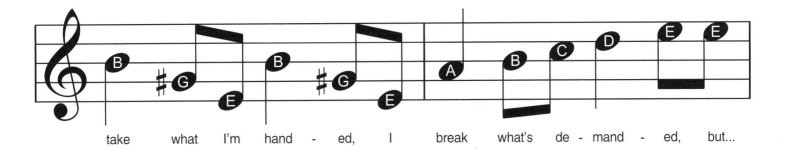

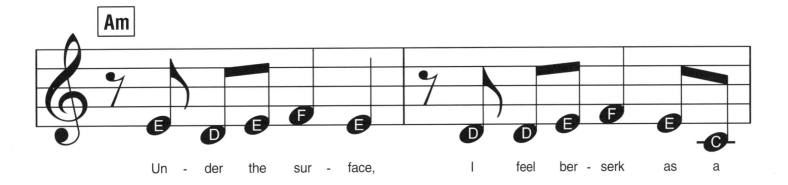

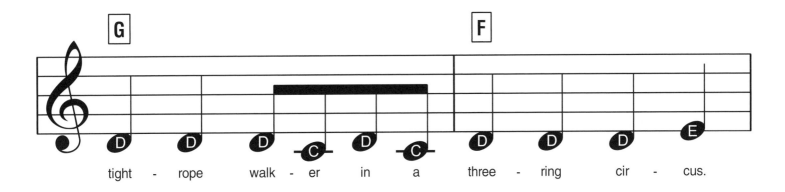

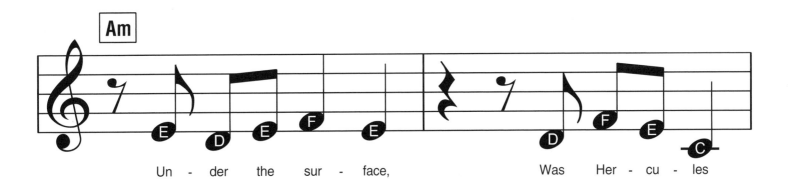

22

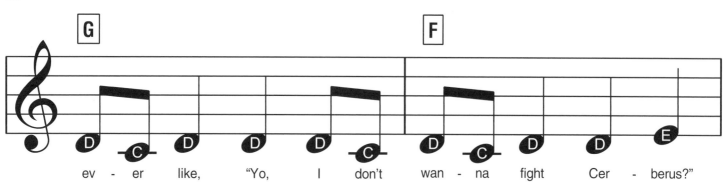

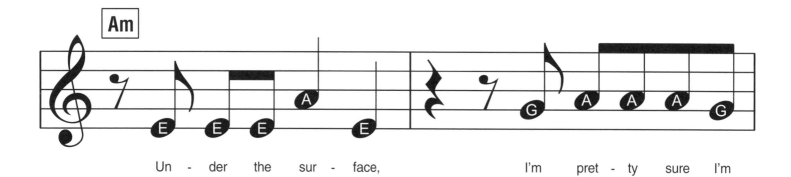

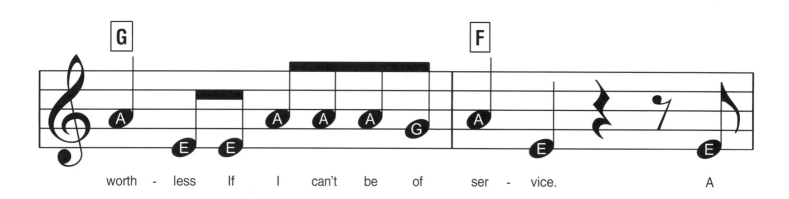

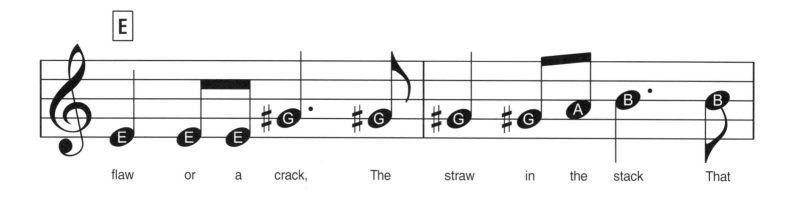

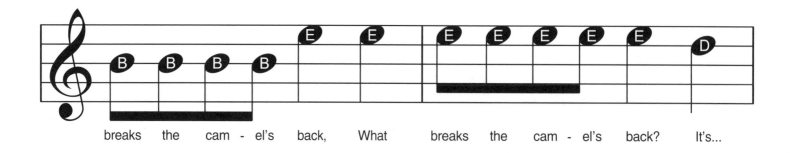

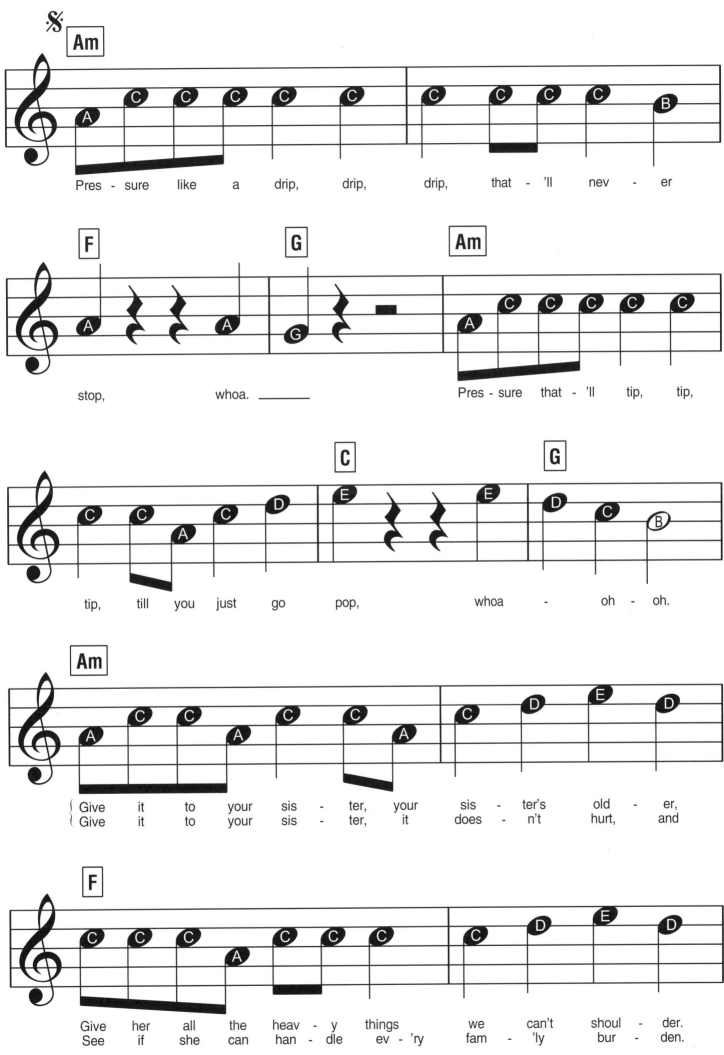

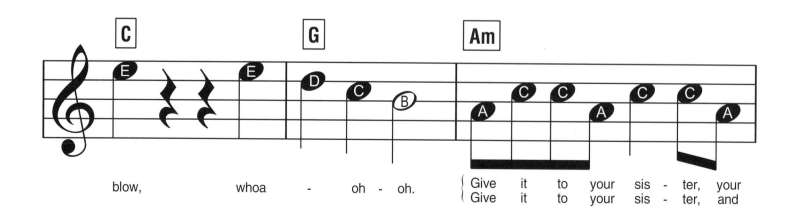

25

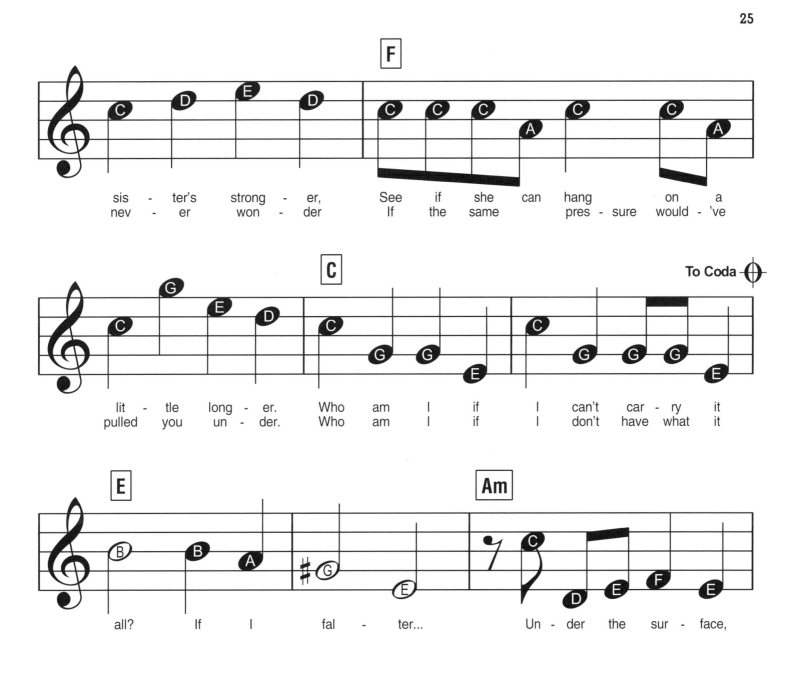

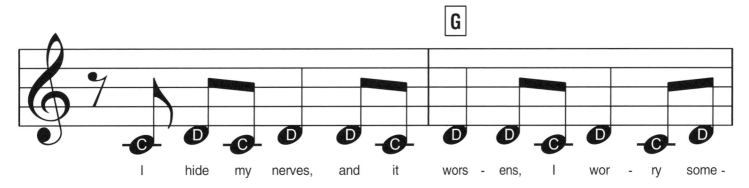

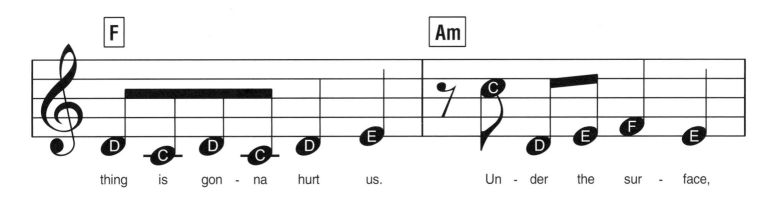

26

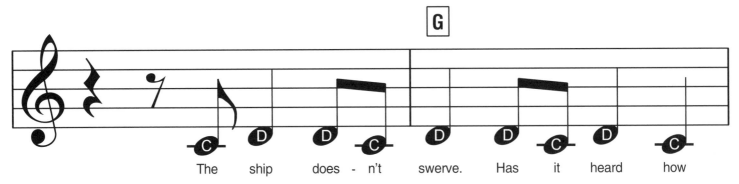

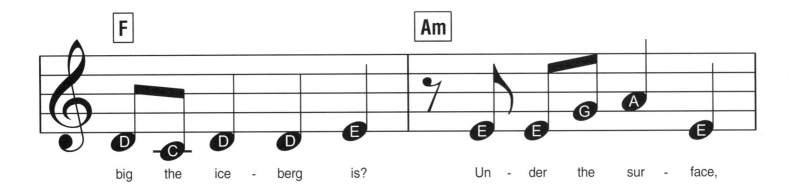

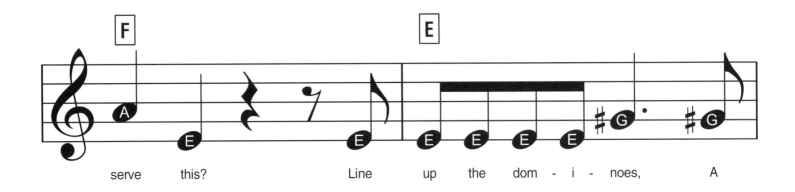

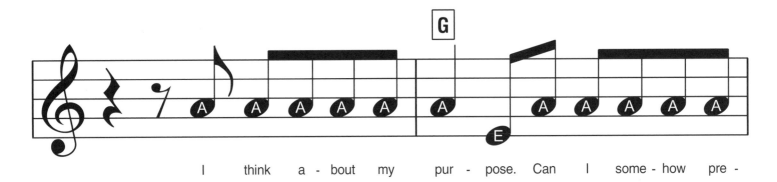

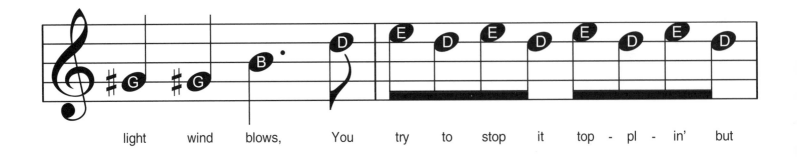

28

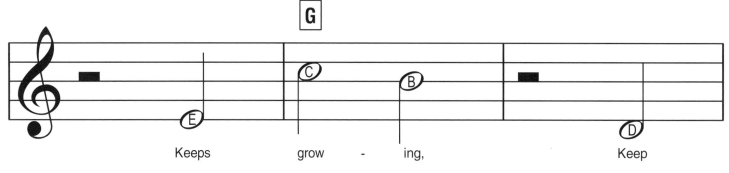

meas - ure   This grow - ing pres - sure.

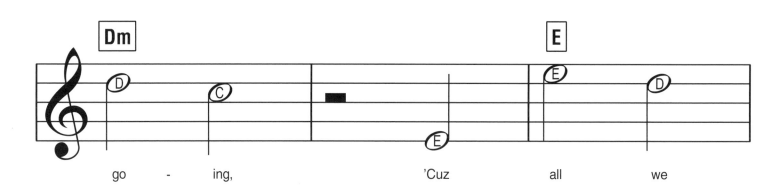

Keeps   grow - ing,   Keep

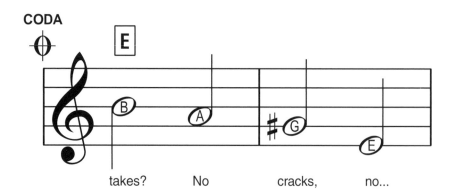

go - ing,   'Cuz   all   we

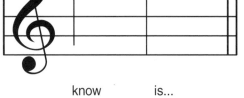

D.S. al Coda
(Return to 𝄉, play to 𝄌
and skip to Coda)

know   is...   takes?   No   cracks,   no...

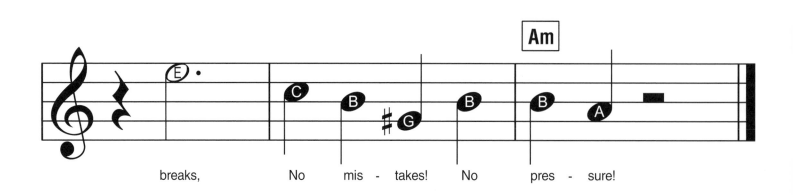

breaks,   No   mis - takes!   No   pres - sure!

Dos Oruguitas

Registration 4
Rhythm: Ballad

Music and Lyrics by
Lin-Manuel Miranda

31

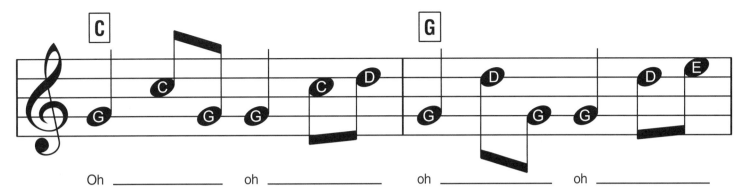

Oh _____ oh _____ oh _____ oh _____

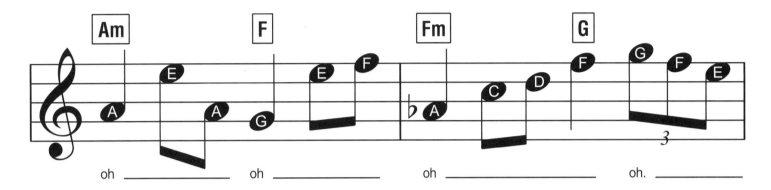

oh _____ oh _____ oh _____ oh. _____

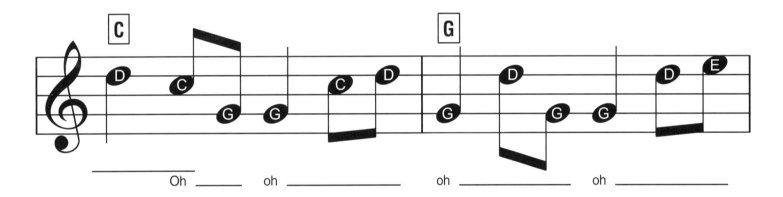

Oh _____ oh _____ oh _____ oh _____

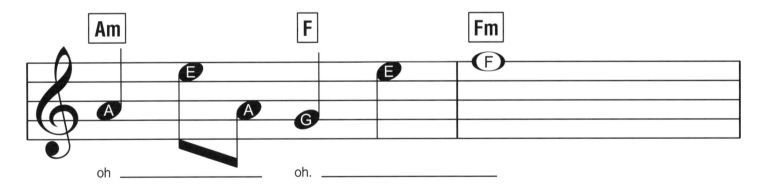

oh _____ oh. _____

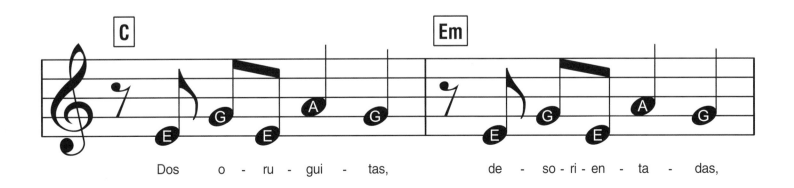

Dos o - ru - gui - tas, de - so - ri - en - ta - das,

33

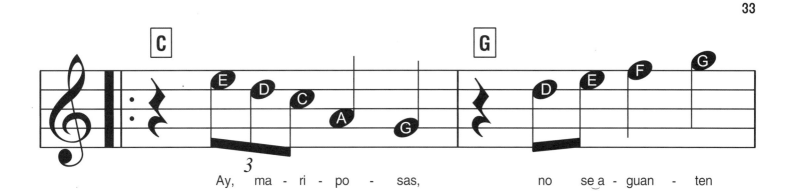

Ay, ma - ri - po - sas,   no se a - guan - ten

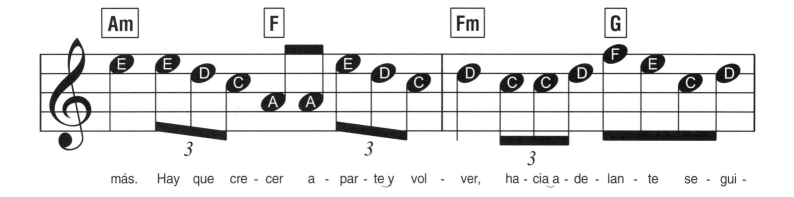

más. Hay que cre - cer a - par - te y vol - ver, ha - cia a - de - lan - te se - gui -

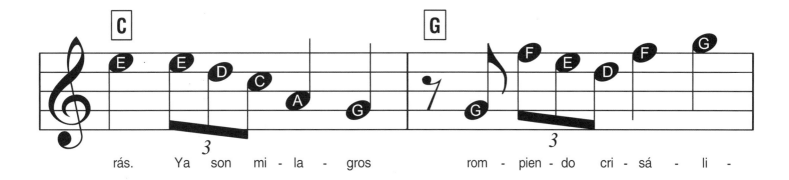

rás.   Ya son mi - la - gros   rom - pien - do cri - sá - li -

Play 3 times

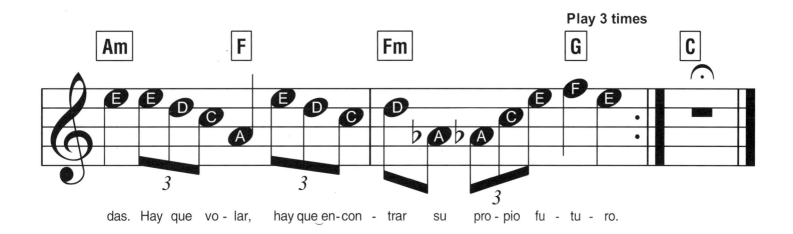

das. Hay que vo - lar, hay que en - con - trar su pro - pio fu - tu - ro.

We Don't Talk About Bruno

Registration 8
Rhythm: Latin or Calypso

Music and Lyrics by
Lin-Manuel Miranda

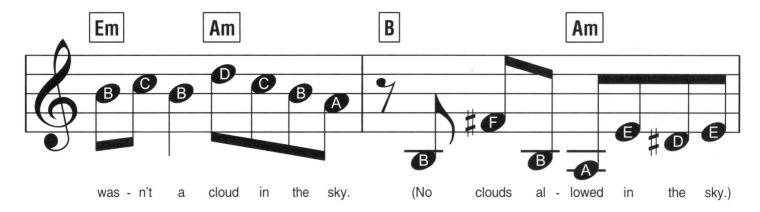

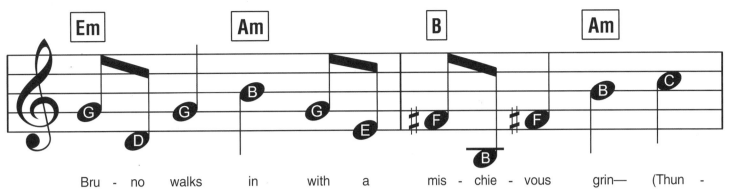

Bru - no walks in with a mis - chie - vous grin— (Thun -

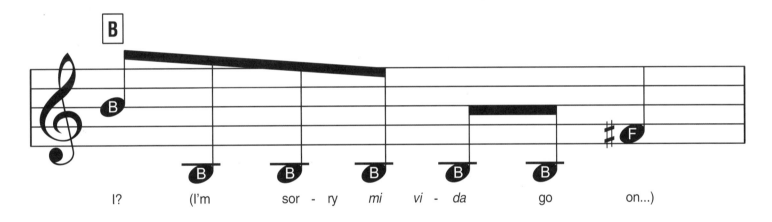

der!!) You tell - ing this sto - ry or am

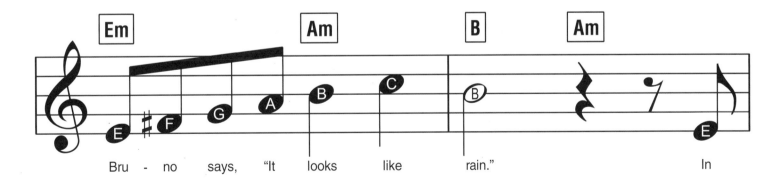

I? (I'm sor - ry *mi vi - da* go on...)

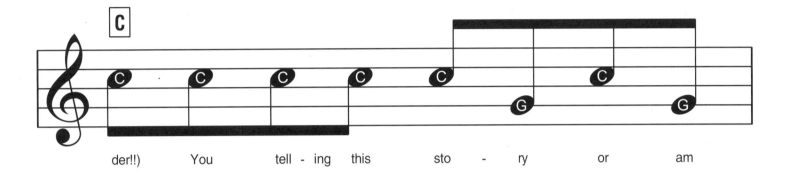

Bru - no says, "It looks like rain." In

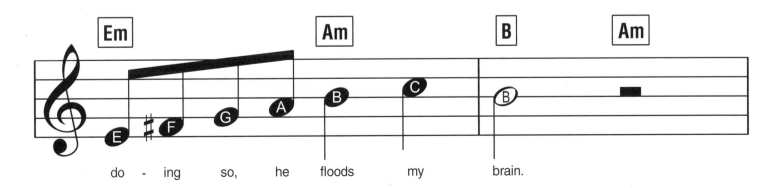

do - ing so, he floods my brain.

36

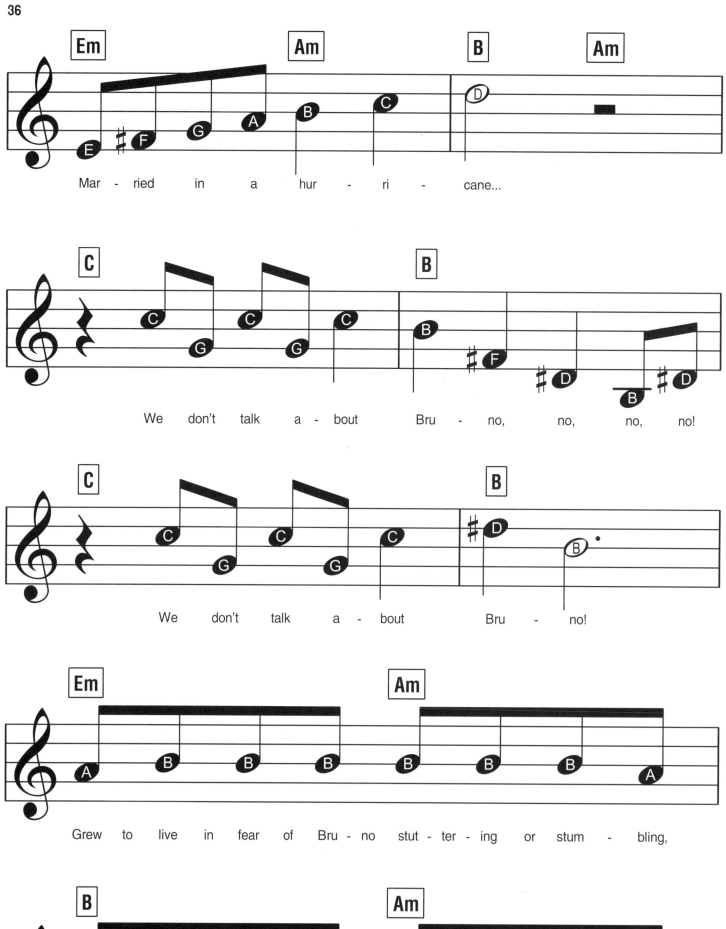

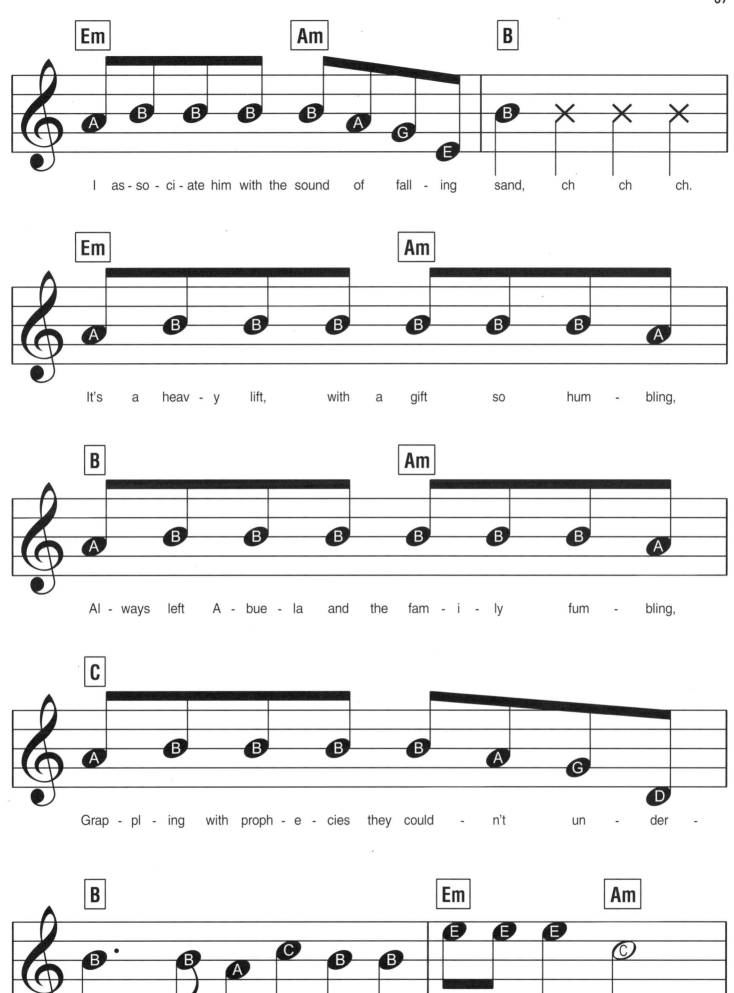

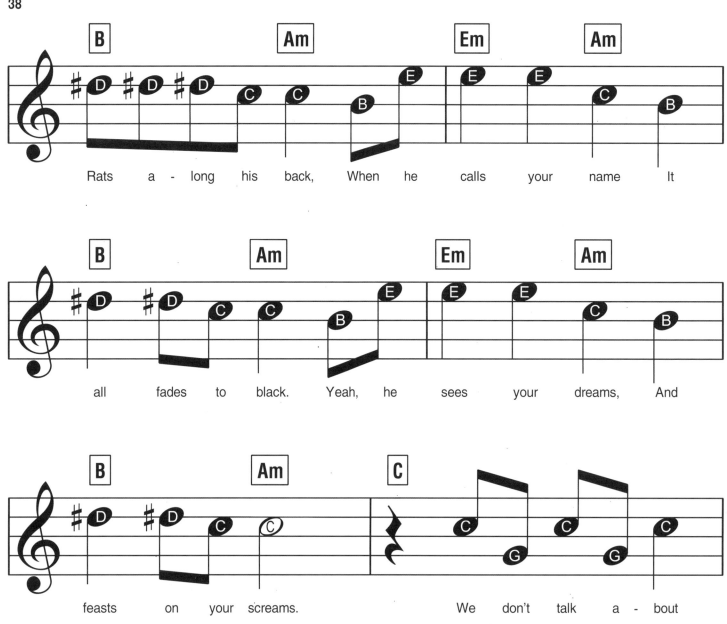

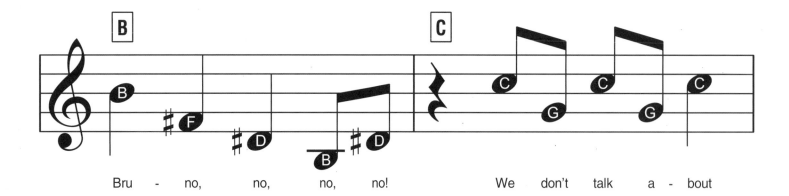

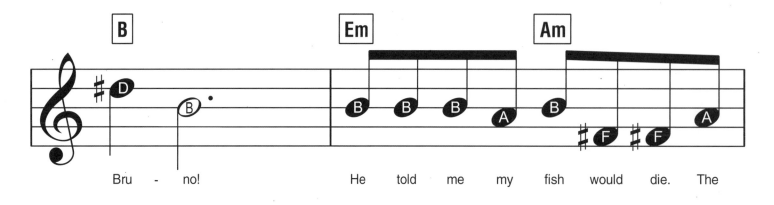

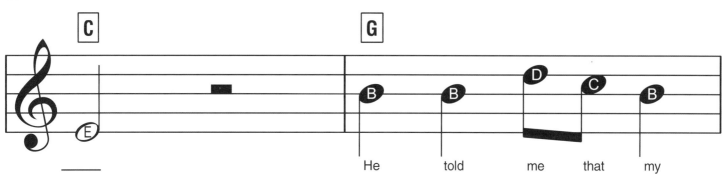

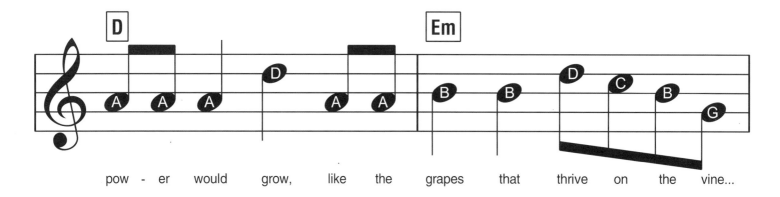

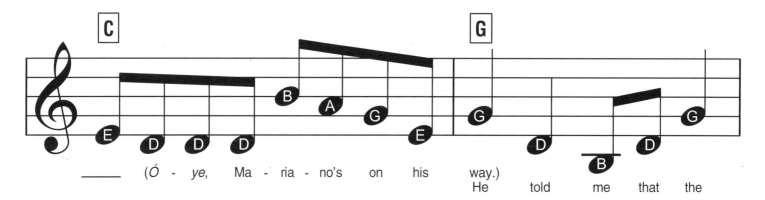

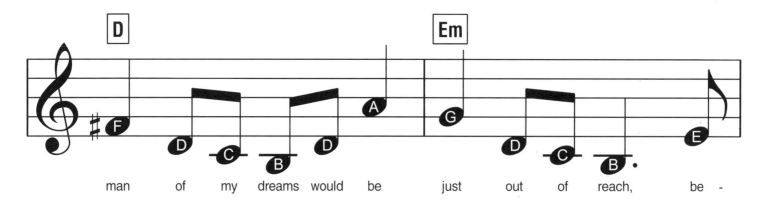

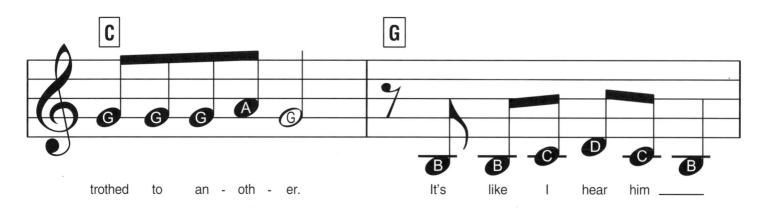

What Else Can I Do?

Registration 2
Rhythm: Pop or Rock

Music and Lyrics by
Lin-Manuel Miranda

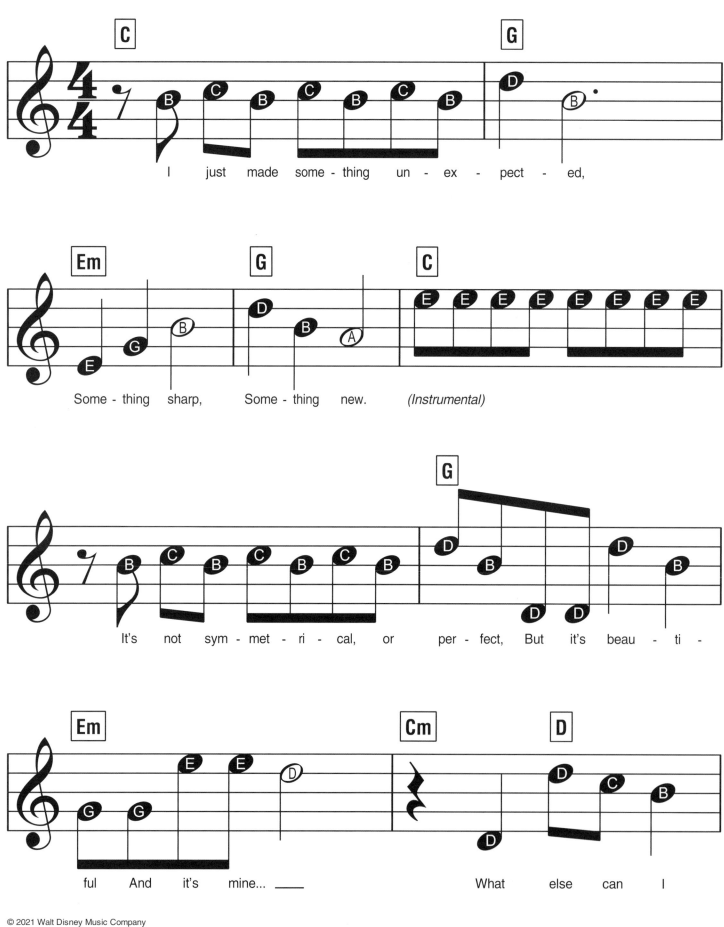

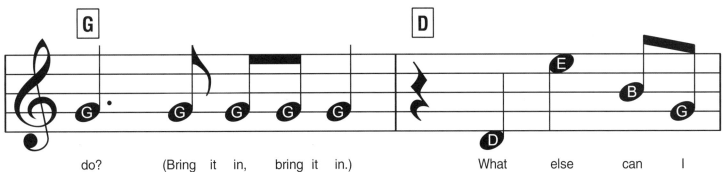

do? (Bring it in, bring it in.) What else can I

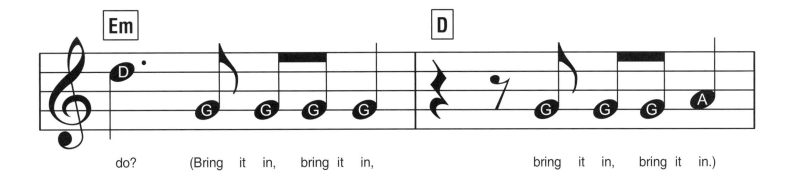

do? (Bring it in, bring it in, bring it in, bring it in.)

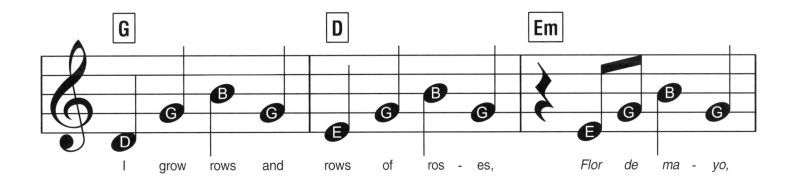

I grow rows and rows of ros - es, *Flor de ma - yo,*

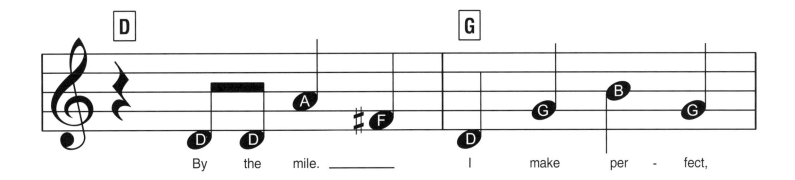

By the mile. _____ I make per - fect,

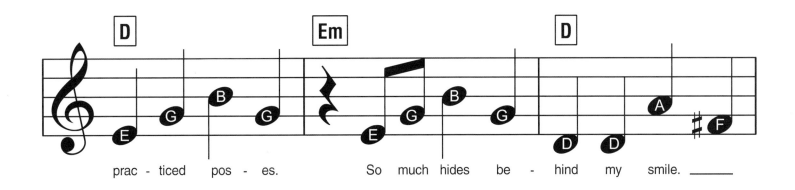

prac - ticed pos - es. So much hides be - hind my smile. _____

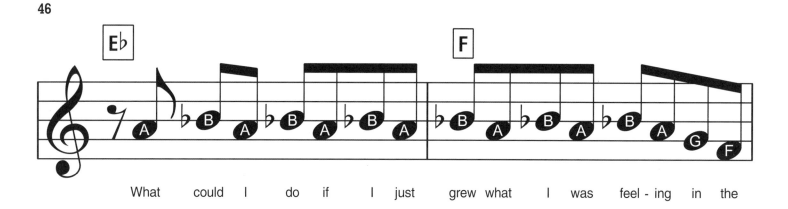

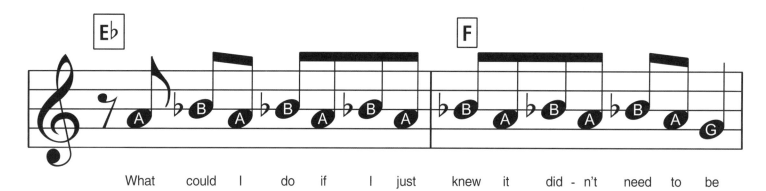

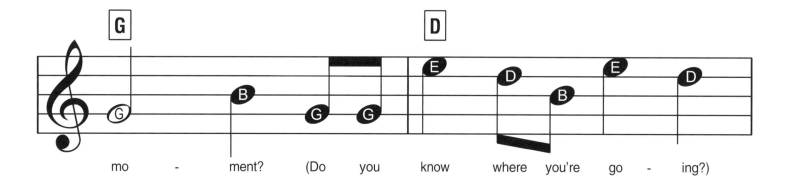

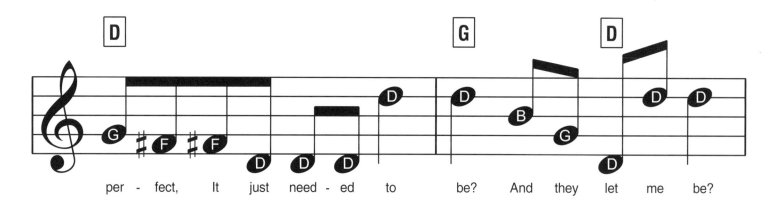

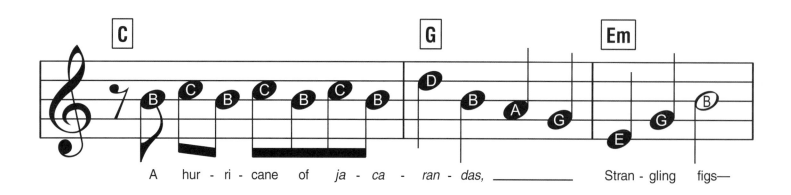

Hang - ing vines— *Pal - ma de ce - ra* fills the air as I _____ climb And I push through... What else can I do? _____ Can I de - liv - er us a riv - er of sun - dew? _____ Care-ful it's car - niv - o - rous, a lit - tle just won't

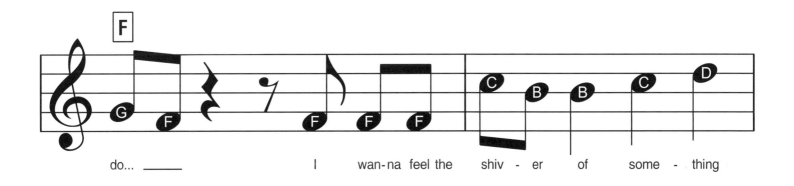

do... _____ I wan-na feel the shiv - er of some - thing

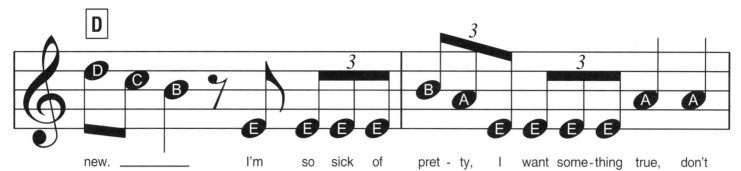

new. _____ I'm so sick of pret - ty, I want some-thing true, don't

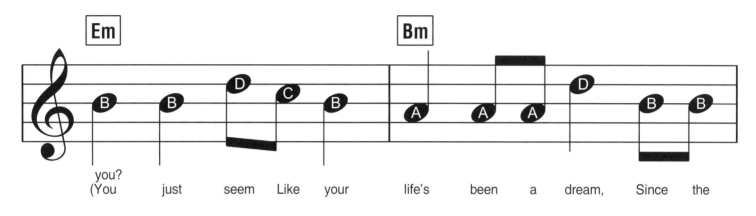

you?
(You just seem Like your life's been a dream, Since the

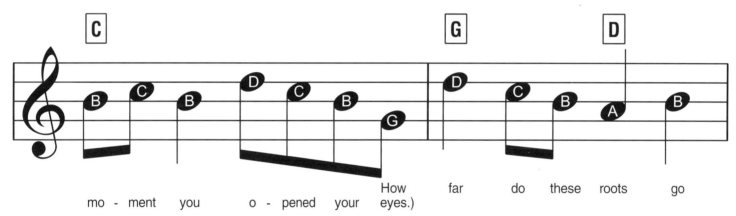

mo - ment you o - pened your eyes.) How far do these roots go

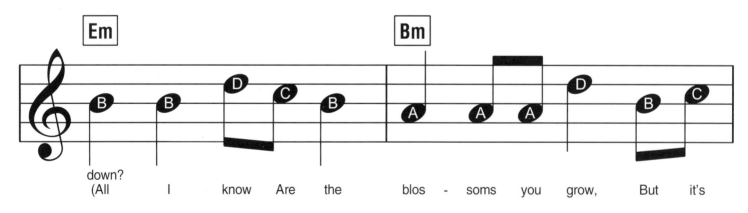

down?
(All I know Are the blos - soms you grow, But it's

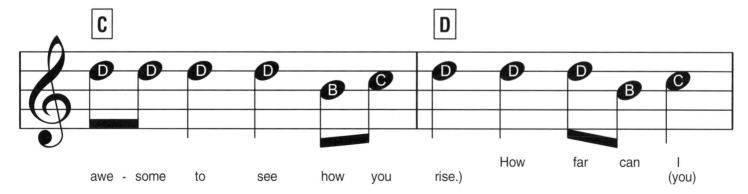

awe - some to see how you rise.) How far can I (you)

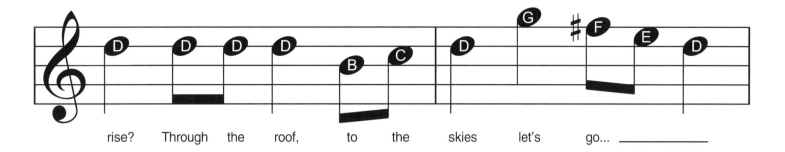

rise? Through the roof, to the skies let's go... _____

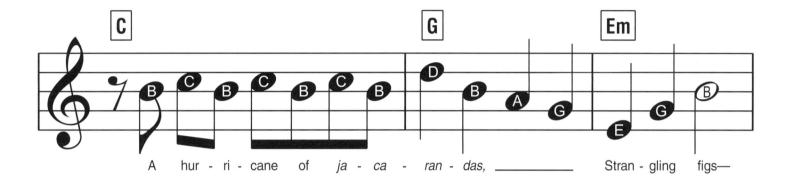

A hur - ri - cane of *ja - ca - ran - das,* _____ Stran - gling figs—

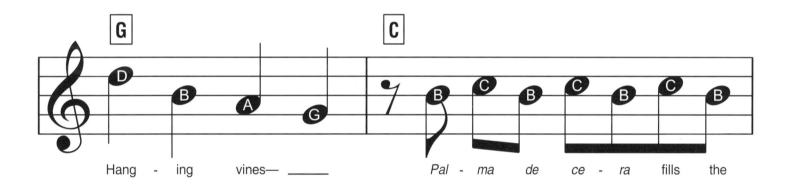

Hang - ing vines— _____ *Pal - ma de ce - ra* fills the

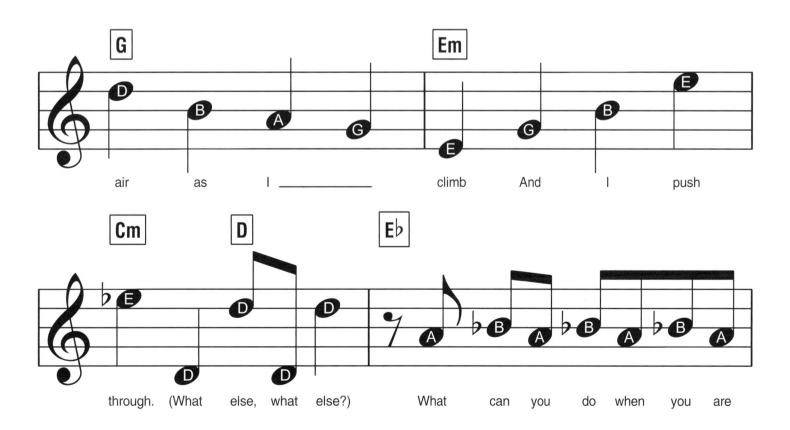

air as I _____ climb And I push

through. (What else, what else?) What can you do when you are

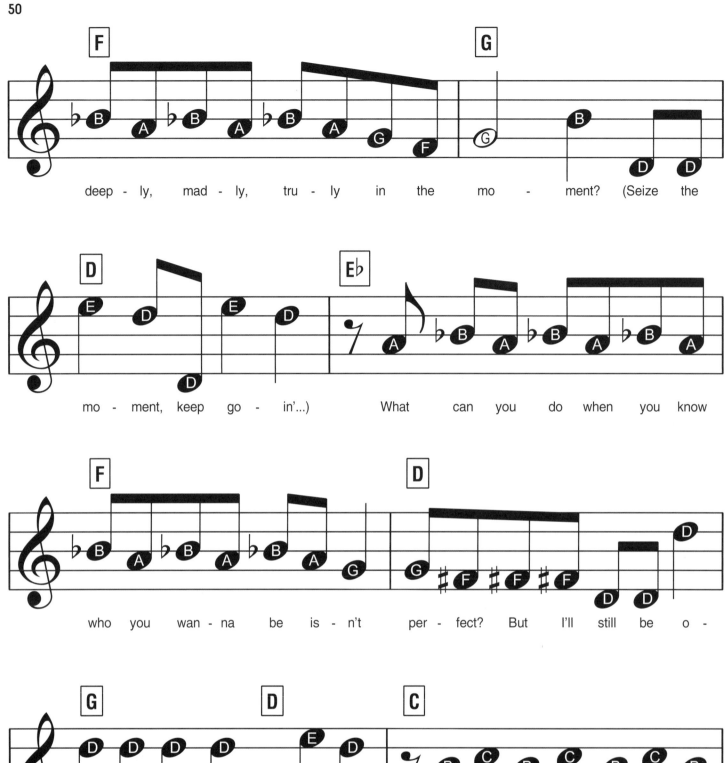

deep - ly, mad - ly, tru - ly in the mo - ment? (Seize the

mo - ment, keep go - in'...) What can you do when you know

who you wan - na be is - n't per - fect? But I'll still be o -

kay? (Hey, ev - 'ry - bod - y, clear the way!) I'm com - ing through with *ta - be -*

bu - ia... _____ Mak - ing waves—

All of You

Registration 4
Rhythm: Latin Pop or Acoustic

Music and Lyrics by
Lin-Manuel Miranda

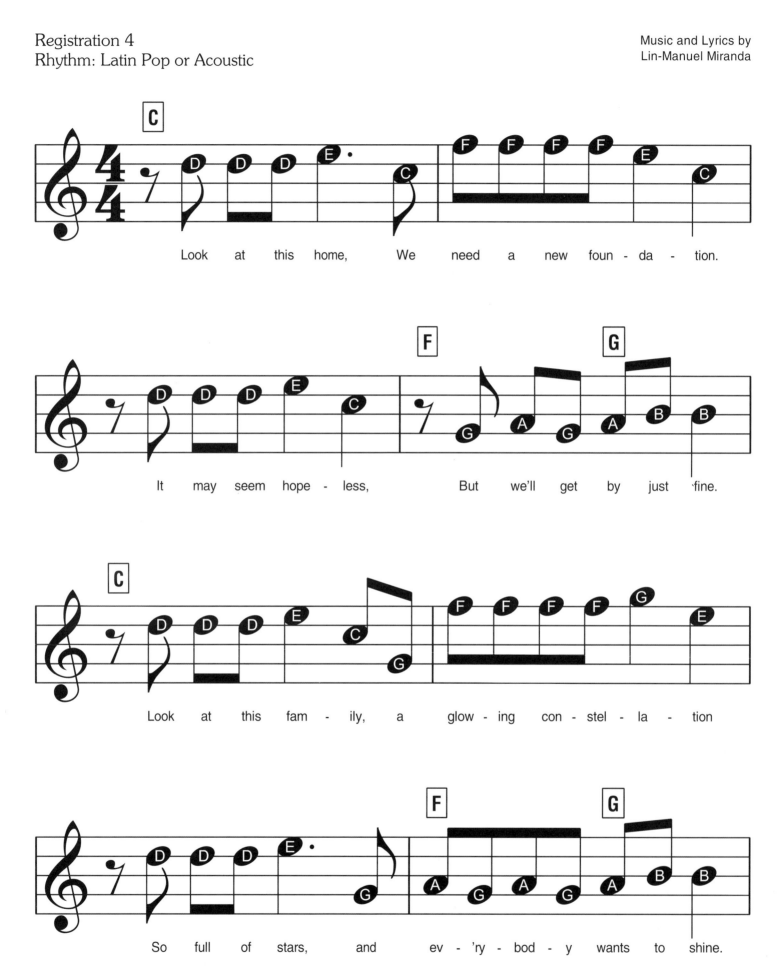

(Instrumental) But the stars don't shine, they burn, And the

con - stel - la - tions shift. I think it's time you

learn: _____ You're more than just your gift. And I'm sor - ry I held

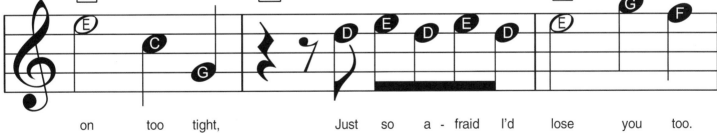

on too tight, Just so a - fraid I'd lose you too.

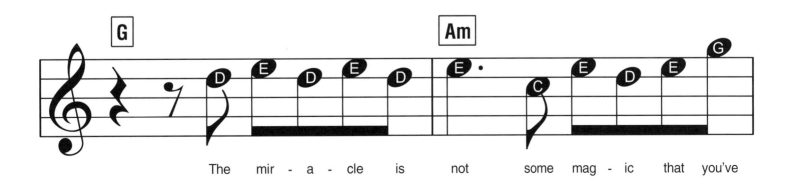

The mir - a - cle is not some mag - ic that you've

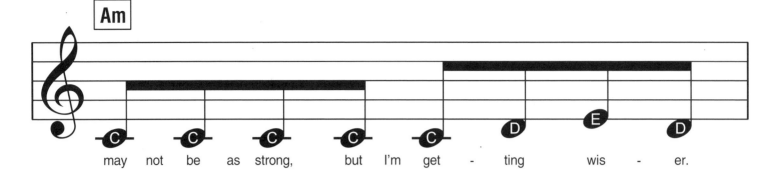

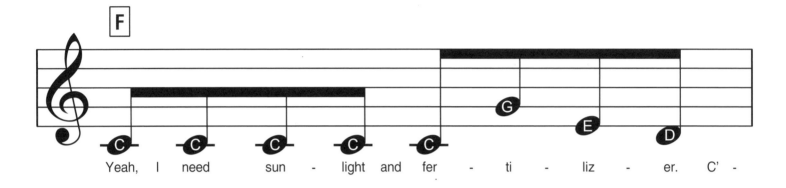

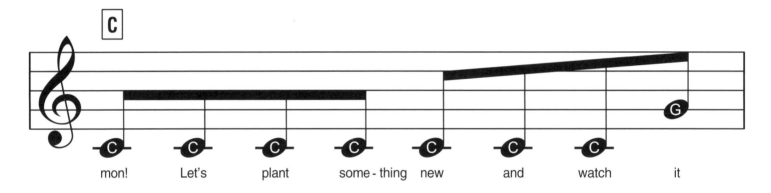

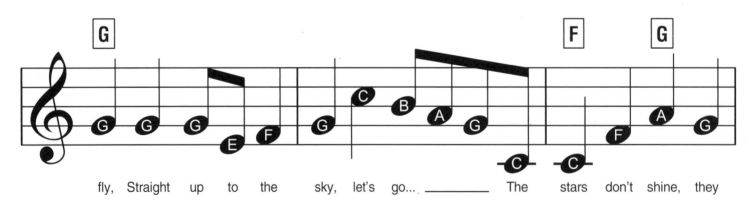

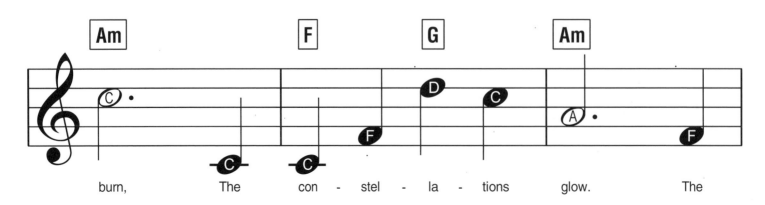

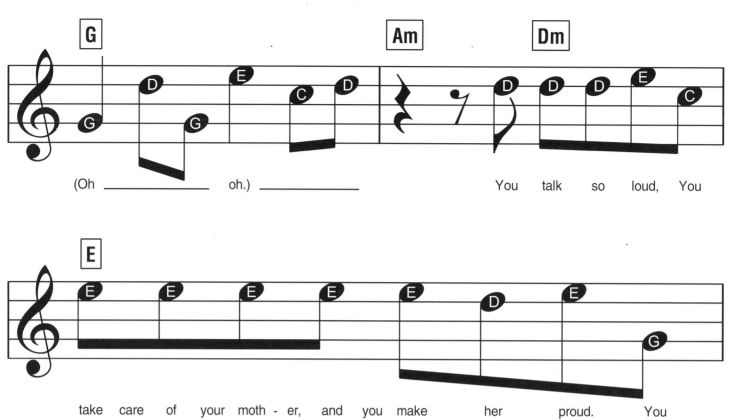

(Oh _____ oh.) _____ You talk so loud, You

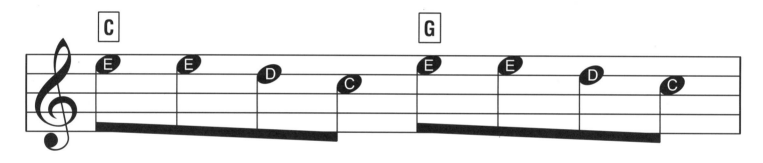

take care of your moth - er, and you make her proud. You

write your own po - et - ry, ev - 'ry night when you go to sleep And I'm

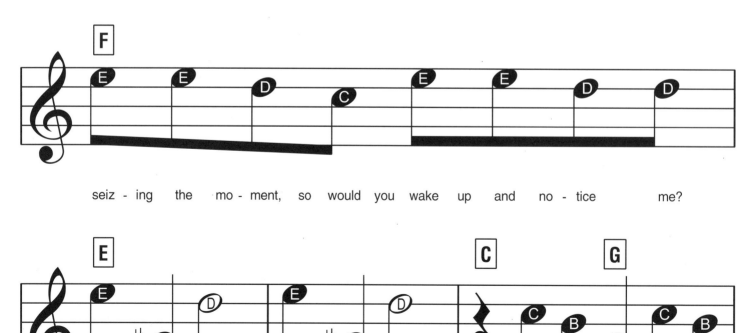

seiz - ing the mo - ment, so would you wake up and no - tice me?

(Instrumental) (All of you, all of

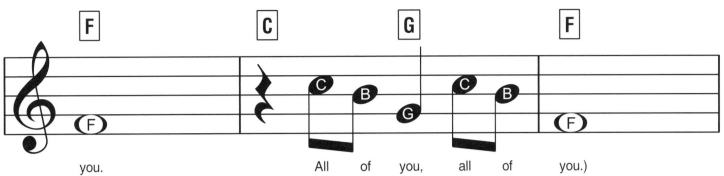

you.   All   of   you,   all   of   you.)

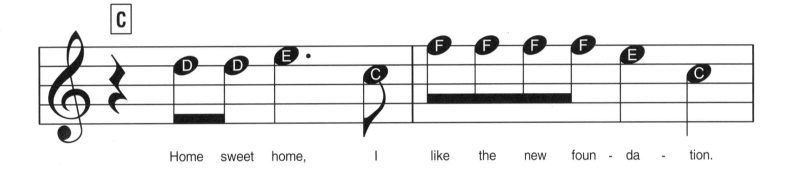

Home   sweet   home,   I   like   the   new   foun - da - tion.

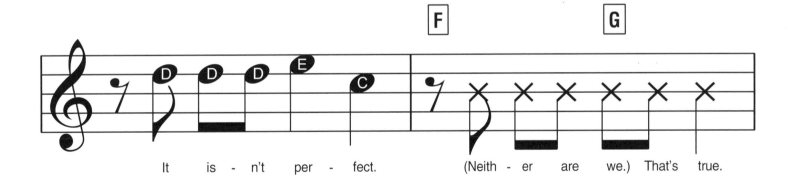

It   is - n't   per - fect.   (Neith - er   are   we.)   That's   true.

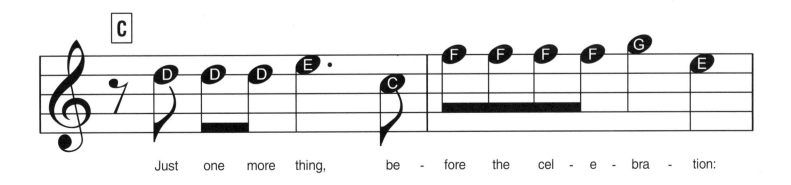

Just   one   more   thing,   be - fore   the   cel - e - bra - tion:

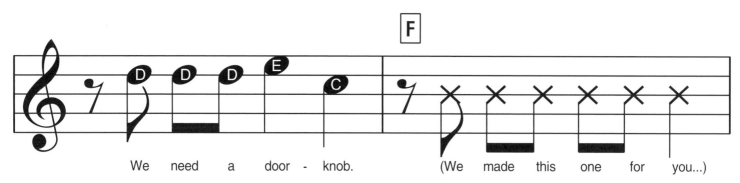

We need a door - knob. (We made this one for you...)

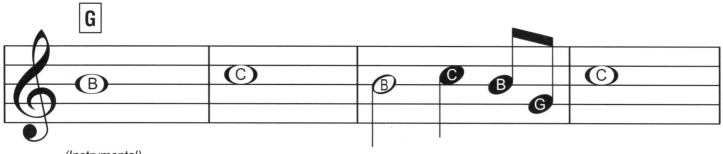

(Instrumental)

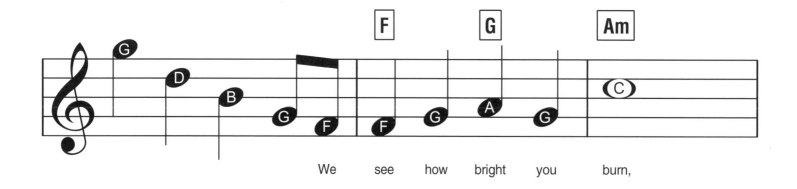

We see how bright you burn,

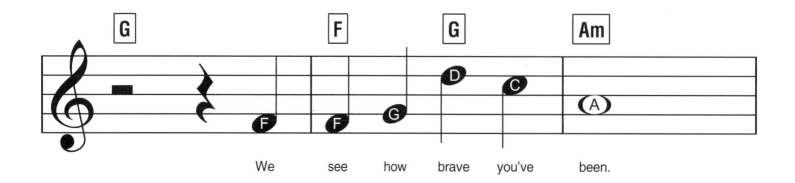

We see how brave you've been.

63

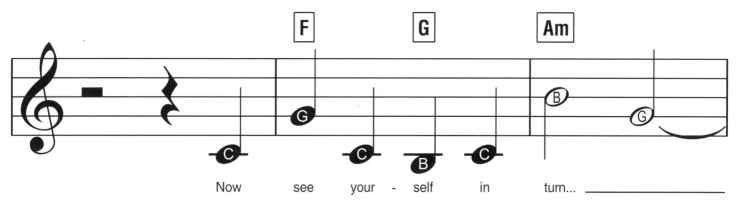

Now see your-self in turn... _____

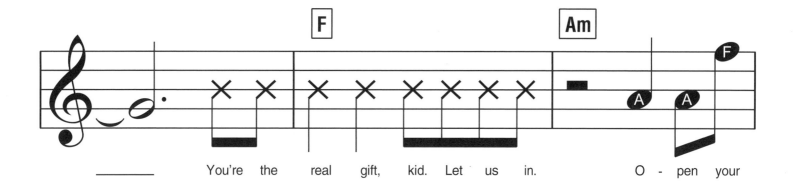

_____ You're the real gift, kid. Let us in. O - pen your

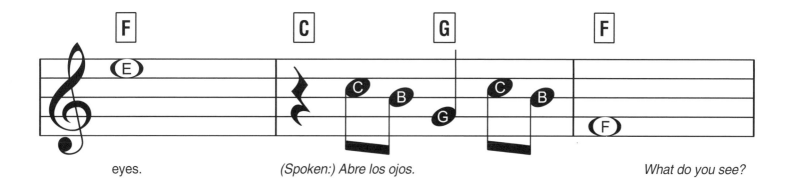

eyes. *(Spoken:) Abre los ojos.* *What do you see?*

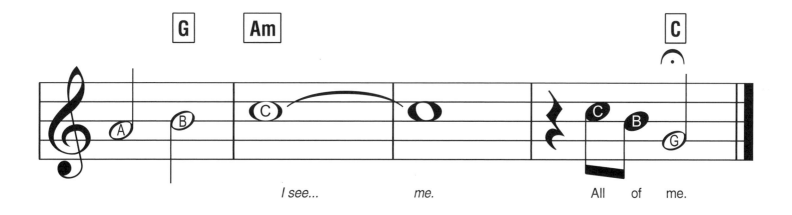

I see... me. All of me.

Colombia, Mi Encanto

Registration 10
Rhythm: Latin or Salsa

Music and Lyrics by
Lin-Manuel Miranda

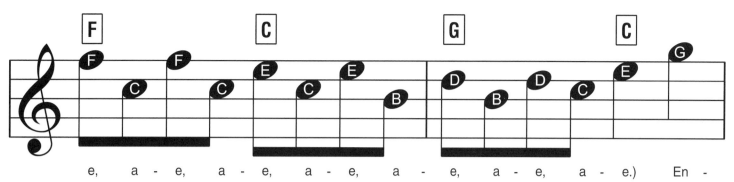

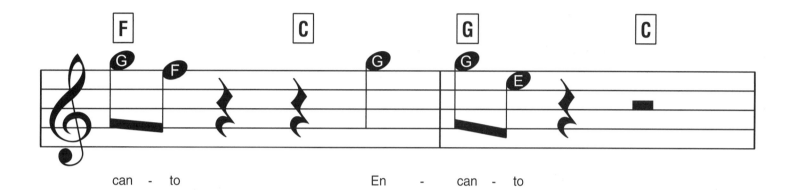

e, a - e, a - e, a - e, a - e, a - e, a - e.) En -

can - to   En - can - to

Co - lom-bia, te qui - e - ro tan - to. (Whoa oh oh oh oh)

Que siem-pre me en-a-mo - ra tu en - can - to. (Whoa oh oh oh oh)

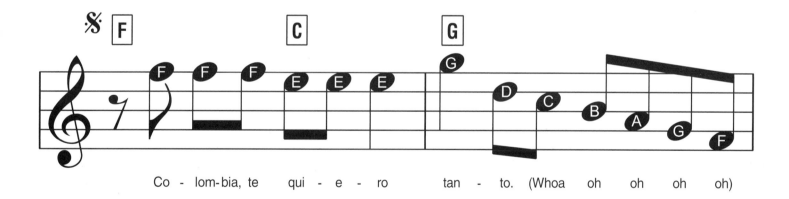

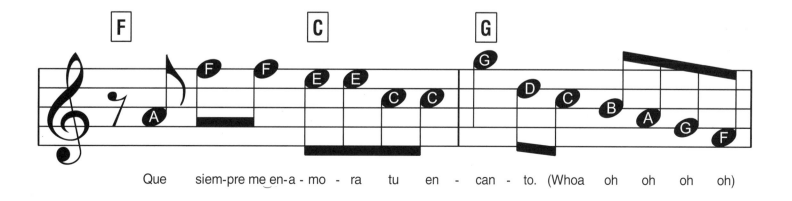

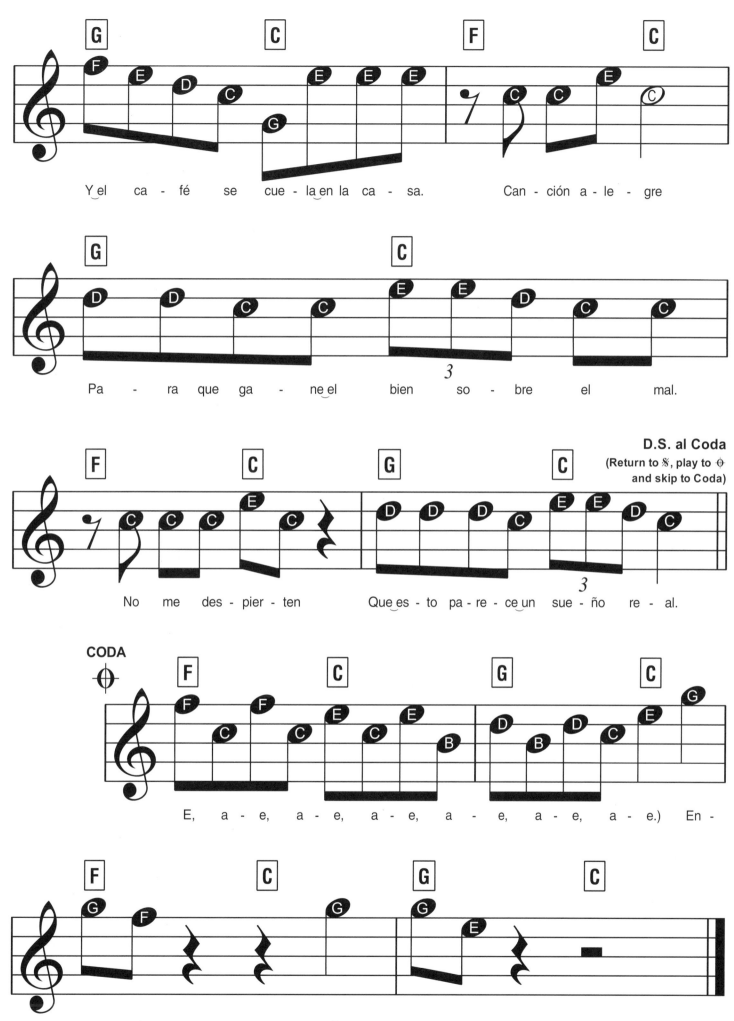

Two Oruguitas

Registration 4
Rhythm: Ballad

Music and Lyrics by
Lin-Manuel Miranda

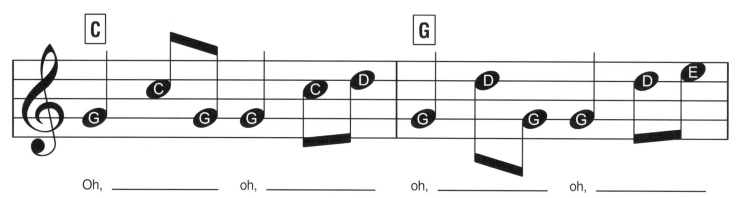

Oh, _____ oh, _____ oh, _____ oh, _____

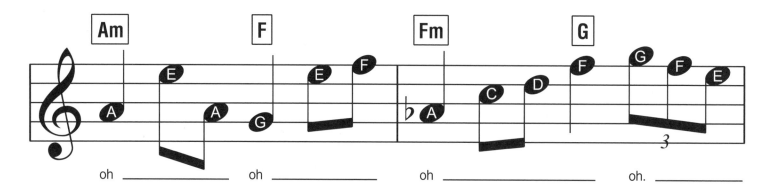

oh _____ oh _____ oh _____ oh. _____

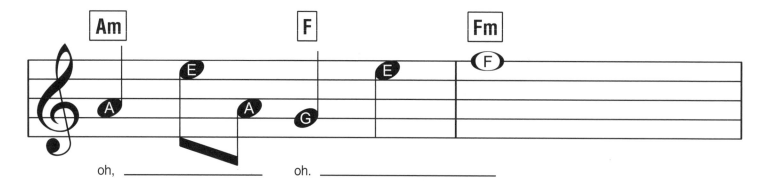

Oh _____ oh _____ oh _____ oh _____

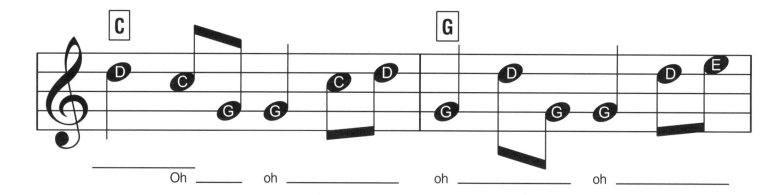

oh, _____ oh. _____

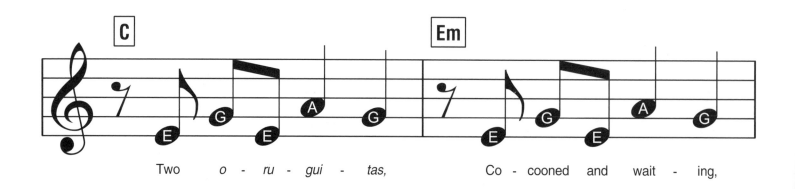

Two *o - ru - gui - tas,*   Co - cooned and wait - ing,

Ay, ma - ri - po - sas,   Don't you hold on too

tight. Both of you know It's your time to go, To fly a - part, to re - u -

nite. Won - ders sur - round you,   Just let the walls come

down. Don't look be - hind you, Fly 'til you

Play 3 times

find Your way toward to - mor - row.